A neuroscience-based infographic for coaching co[aches]
unable to progress, despite logically understan[ding]

When who *you are* is not embracing who *you* want to be

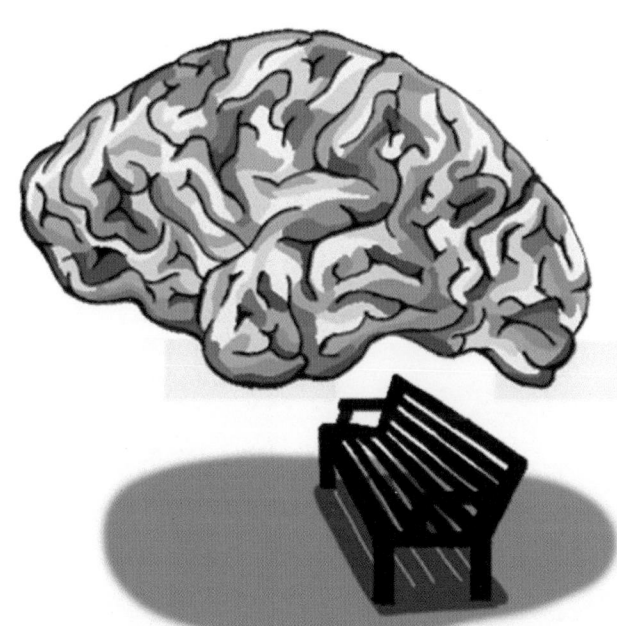

How reflexive hindering curbs a coachee's progress, what might contribute to the brain acting in this way and what can help to change that

Dr Deni Lyall

Copyright © Deni Lyall 2024

www.winningperformance.co.uk

The moral right of the author has been asserted.

All rights reserved. No part of this publication may be reproduced, stored in a retrieval system, or transmitted in any form by any means: graphic, electronic, or mechanical, photocopying, recording or otherwise without the prior permission of the copywrite owner.

Front cover illustration: Will Lyall

Acknowledgements

I want to acknowledge the time and feedback that was so generously given by the executive coaches who participated in my doctoral research. Their experience and thoughts have enabled me to enhance the infographic, its supporting information and to create the MERE Coaching Conversation steps. I am deeply grateful for their enthusiasm, critique and support, all of which have enriched the material in this book.

My doctoral supervisors Prof. Annette Fillery-Travis and Prof. Paul Brown were also fundamental to the rigor underpinning this material. Thank you for your thought-provoking conversation, support and challenge. Finally, I want to thank my coaching supervision group and my husband, Mark, for their enthusiastic confidence in my endeavour to complete this book. In particular Lynda Freeman and Mark for their feedback and suggestions from reading the draft copy. Their comments were much appreciated.

Contents:

1. Introduction
    - how to use this book

Part 1:

3. Infographic to use with a coachee
    - the four sections

12. Reflexive hindering
    - definition and how it manifests in coaching

16. 'Be realistic about your brain'
    - Infographic section in detail

23. 'Our responses are influenced by our past experiences and neurobiology'
    - Infographic section in detail

31. 'Change is possible and takes commitment'
    - Infographic section in detail

Part 2:

36. What can help to change the situation
    - MERE Coaching Conversations
    - Mastering
    - Enabling
    - Realising
    - Embedding

44. References and other resources

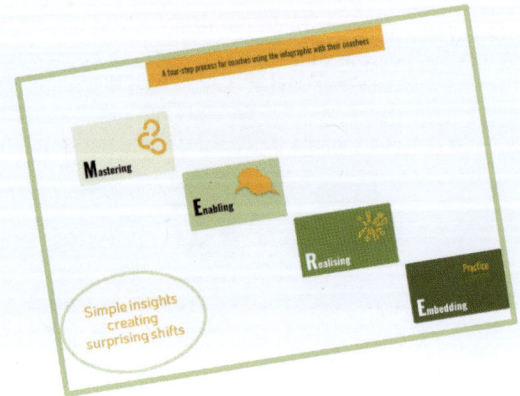

Introduction:

This book is written for coaches and coachees - specifically for when a coachee really wants to change but are somehow hindering their own progress. This behaviour is not deliberate, it is more akin to, *who they are is not embracing who they want to be* and therefore tries to maintain the status-quo. Perhaps the coachee:
- Keeps reverting back to their usual behaviour
- Is stuck on something that they say they want to change
- Realises that they are getting in the way of their own progress but does not know how to change that
- Understands what they need to do, but only attempts simple actions because change feels difficult
- Is unable to quell the doubts, concerns, nervousness or anxiety they have (typically related to what might happen if they took their chosen actions) because those thoughts and feelings appear valid

If so, they could be hampered by a coaching phenomenon I have called *reflexive hindering*. This is when their "tricky brain" (so called by Prof. Paul Gilbert, 2014) creates responses that are misplaced in an attempt to ensure the person survives and thrives in some way. This happens because those responses have been slow to change across the years and have remained the default habit, even though they are outdated. My research demonstrates that for these coachees appreciating some fundamentals of the brain can give them a different perspective on the responses that curb their progress. The infographic in this book was created for that purpose and has been designed with a beginning, middle and end, so that it tells a story. It uses explanatory, rather than overly scientific, terms and is comprehensively referenced. It was used by the executive coaches participating in the research and they found, that for them, it created an insightful conversation that they believed was beneficial to the coachee in some or all of the following ways.

- Real insights that make a difference
- An explanatory understanding of brain function that makes it real
- Invigorates a commitment for action
- Puts a focus on being kind to yourself and others
- Creating a subject to object shift enabling a more detached view
- Belief or hope that change could happen

The executive coaches participating in the research also said that they gained many of the following benefits from using the infographic.

- Created an immersive and informative neurobiological exploration
- Enabled different conversations
- Gave credibility to the coach's neuroscience conversation
- Can be an easy-to-use neuroscience-based tool
- Useful structure and aide-memoir
- A deeper understanding of neuroscience

I have designed this book because I believe that it is worth the coach and coachee understanding more about the concept of reflexive hindering, especially as the responses created by it can feel unquestionable and innate. Part 1 of this book is designed to do that and to create the benefits stated above. Part 2 is designed to give coaches a process for successfully using the infographic with their coachees. It contains four steps and was created using the best practice gained from the executive coaches who used the infographic during the research.

How to use this book:

Part 1 is written for coaches and coachees. It covers the infographic and the information underlying each of its elements.

Part 2 is written for coaches and is intended to help them successfully use the infographic with their coachees to achieve the same benefits that the executive coaches achieved with their coachees during the research.

Using Part 1 – coach and coachee

Pages 4-11 are the four infographic sections and are for the coach to use with their coachee during the coaching session. Each section has its own page so you can work through each section individually.

Pages 12-35 give the information underlying each element on the infographic. This is the information the coach will want to have familiarised themselves with before they share the infographic pages with their coachee. It can be useful for the coachee to read these pages after the coach has had that conversation with them.

Using Part 2 - coach

Pages 36-38 overview of the MERE Coaching Conversation steps.

Pages 39-43 go through each step. They contain tips and advice on how make the infographic-based conversation insightful and valuable to a reflexively-hindered coachee.

References & other resources

Page 44 suggests resources that give a useful overview of the brain and the field of neuroscience, as well as the references for reflexive hindering. There are a number of books, articles, websites, etc listed here if the coach or coachee would like to gain a general overview of the brain and the field of neuroscience. They are a thought-provoking read in many ways. **If you only want to read one book, I would suggest 'How the mind works' by Pinker. I would also encourage a coach to read 'Neuro' by Rose & Abi-Rached as it is a good insight into the field of neuroscience.**

Pages 45-47 list the cross-referencing and other specific resources for pages 17-43. The specific references supporting each element of the infographic are listed here. There are other references than those listed on these pages, but the ones noted felt most suitable to include. These pages also contain a variety of other resources (pertinent to a particular element) that bring the element to life in many ways, including videos, articles, online talks, websites, etc. Some of these resources can be used by the coach, with their coachee, to help illustrate aspects on the infographic. For example, the 'Colour Changing Card Trick' (R Wiseman, 2012) is a useful and short video to watch with your coachee.

Pages 47-49 give the full reference details.

Part 1 – The Infographic

A useful aide-memoir

Simple insights creating surprising shifts

Which characteristics of reflexive hindering resonate for you?

When *who you are* is not embracing *who you want to be*

Reflexive hindering

What contributes to the brain acting in this way and what can help to change that

What insights are you taking from this section?

| It is awesome | Be realistic about your brain | It has limitations |

It is awesome

- Hundreds of types of neurons, neurochemicals and other cells
- In 1mm³, approx. 1bil connection sites, tens of 1000s of neurons & 4km of connecting tissue
- Relatively integrated rather than separately functioning areas

- The brain seeks to repeat what gets rewarded/ to avoid or reduce threat
- Same basic structure as each other & individually modified by experience

- Neurons are like factories: taking in, using, converting, generating and releasing different things
- Humans are a complex system – responses have different probabilities but every action is you

It has limitations

- It's not all-encompassing: illusionists make the most of this
- *Seeing* & *hearing* happen in the brain not in the eyes & ears

- Improves reaction times and conserves energy
- Predicts what is being sensed and updates the difference

- Advantageous aspects survive better
- Evolution takes time, so we are making the best of what we have

Wheel segments: It's busy inside · Not an unquestionable truth · Assumes and Approximates · Evolved not designed · Like a vibrant city · More or less developed by 25 · Centre: "Just doing" managing allostasis

Which aspects from this section are particularly thought-provoking for you?

| How can this happen? | Our responses are influenced by our past experiences and our neurobiology | What happens? |

Developed to ensure you survive and thrive

Early memories and traumatic events ...
... can feel *real* when triggered

Habits conserve energy: life is a series of habits.
"Better safe than sorry" approach to threat

Brains are complex wet-systems so,
irrelevant inputs can get linked to major events

Memories get altered over time,
and can be triggered by weak associations

All inputs go into our brain to varying degrees,
thus we can react to nonconscious stimuli

Humans have expanded the definition of threat ...
to social threats such as humiliation and "likes"

Safe & Threat responses
Stephen Porges

Safe mode
Curious, compassionate, connected to others
Able to problem solve, be creative
Inhibited threat response, smiling
 Socially Engage

Fight / Flight mode
Aggressive, frustration, anxiety, fear
Reduced thinking & immune system
Sensitive to threats
Motionless face
 Mobilise

Freeze mode
Overwhelm, helplessness, feeling trapped
Withdrawn, *robot like* – do as told
Reduced social awareness
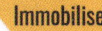 Immobilise

What action or change would make the most difference towards progressing your coaching goals?

| Is it possible? | Change is possible and takes commitment | How could I do it? |

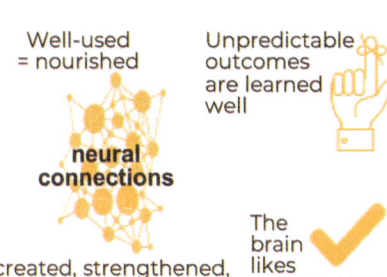

- constantly adapt

- to enhance learning & thinking

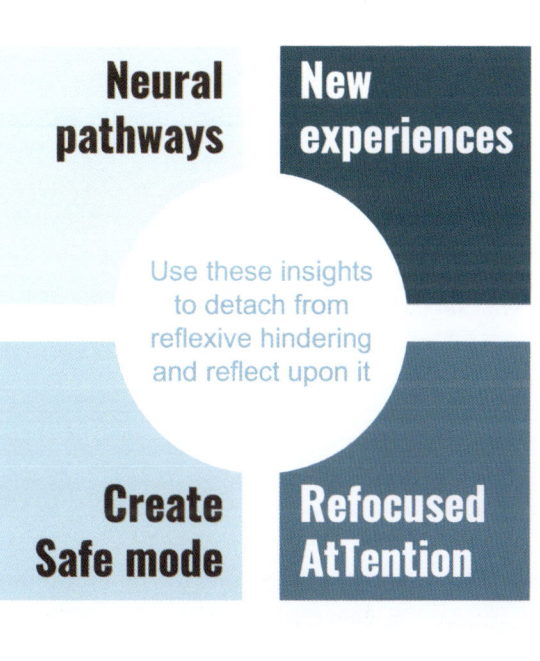

Use these insights to detach from reflexive hindering and reflect upon it

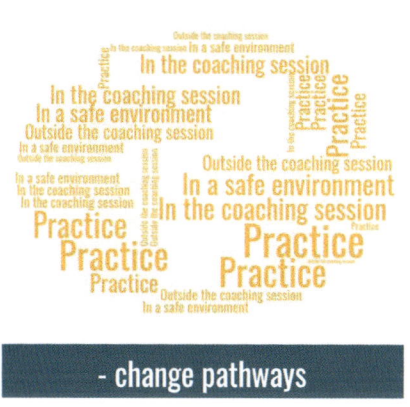

- change pathways

- is a useful distraction method

When *who you are* is not embracing *who you want to be*

Reflexive hindering

Occasionally some coachees seem unable to progress despite logically understanding the actions they could take, even though they are motivated to participate in the coaching programme. Although their desired behaviours are natural to other people, it appears that at some level they question or fear whether they can also act in these ways. Thus, their nonconscious response is to curb their attempts at trying to change their current behaviour.

This inaction, reduced motivation to take actions or avoidance of actions that could be helpful, is neither conscious nor planned. It does however result in a state in which coachees seem unable to act in a manner that is directed towards achieving the coaching goals. This is called 'reflexive hindering'.

Sometimes a coachee becomes fused with their responses, which makes the responses seem unquestionably obvious and pertinent. This makes it difficult for coachees to be objective and to think about how to advance their coaching goals. Research has shown that understanding some pertinent fundamentals of the brain can be beneficial in these situations.

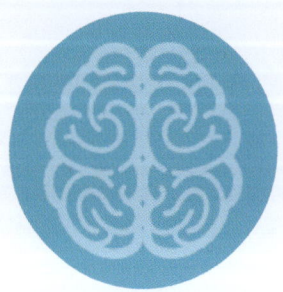

How reflexive hindering manifests during coaching

Constraining various conversations and actions: Reflexive hindering can manifest itself in various ways during a coaching programme: extensively across a programme; only whilst discussing a certain coaching goal; during particular coaching conversations or whilst attempting actions outside of the coaching session. It shows up as a growing cautiousness towards discussing possibilities and developing options for action. As reflexive hindering intensifies, it progressively hampers the ability to take meaningful actions, thus hindering progress towards the desired coaching objectives. The responses become *reality* and as they intensify, the espoused actions seem less conceivable. Eventually reflexive hindering can constrain the ability to adapt further.

Unable to fully detach from the response: Most coachees rationally understand that some of their thoughts and behaviours hamper their ability to achieve their coaching goals. Coachees also know that in order to progress their coaching outcomes they need to be able to change in some way. However, when reflexive hindering is present, a coachee may lose that objectivity as the deep-seated responses are *real* and *pertinent* for them. For the coachee, the situation is threatening although they may struggle to articulate why. Thus, that coachee becomes fused with their experience at that moment, unable to detach and become objective. This makes exploration, reflection and action towards advancing the coaching goals more difficult. A reflexively-hindered coachee might:

- display bafflement as to the reason why they cannot progress, even though they appreciate their predicament.
- be unaware of how they are impeding their own progress as their actions appear congruent to them.
- state that all the options explored thus far are implausible, although they struggle to articulate why.

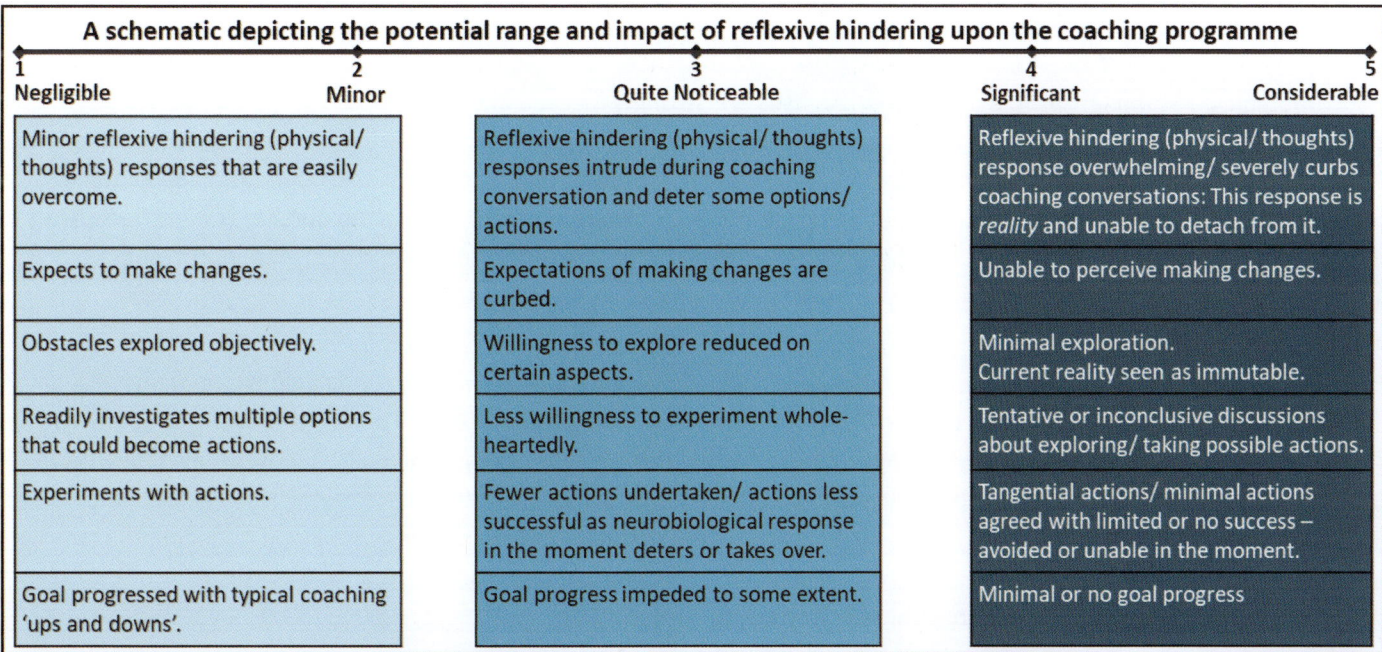

A schematic depicting the potential range and impact of reflexive hindering upon the coaching programme

1 Negligible	2 Minor	3 Quite Noticeable	4 Significant	5 Considerable
Minor reflexive hindering (physical/ thoughts) responses that are easily overcome.		Reflexive hindering (physical/ thoughts) responses intrude during coaching conversation and deter some options/ actions.	Reflexive hindering (physical/ thoughts) response overwhelming/ severely curbs coaching conversations: This response is *reality* and unable to detach from it.	
Expects to make changes.		Expectations of making changes are curbed.	Unable to perceive making changes.	
Obstacles explored objectively.		Willingness to explore reduced on certain aspects.	Minimal exploration. Current reality seen as immutable.	
Readily investigates multiple options that could become actions.		Less willingness to experiment whole-heartedly.	Tentative or inconclusive discussions about exploring/ taking possible actions.	
Experiments with actions.		Fewer actions undertaken/ actions less successful as neurobiological response in the moment deters or takes over.	Tangential actions/ minimal actions agreed with limited or no success – avoided or unable in the moment.	
Goal progressed with typical coaching 'ups and downs'.		Goal progress impeded to some extent.	Minimal or no goal progress	

What contributes to the brain acting this way - neurobiological context of reflexive hindering

Our formative years: People are often unaware of how accepting they are of their interpretation of the world, their norms and beliefs, and how this affects their actions. These become unquestionable truths that have been unknowingly learnt from their upbringing. The aspects of the brain responsible for such perceptions and responses are neurobiologically constructed during someone's formative years, when the person is developing and learning how to survive in the world. These neurobiological patterns emerge as the way of navigating life in order to adapt, survive and thrive. These neural pathways are then responsible for embracing change when it is perceived as a natural evolution of who that person is, and that its consequences are perceived as being acceptable. However, when the change is perceived (consciously or nonconsciously) as being beyond that natural evolution, and its consequences seem less viable, a deep-seated reaction occurs to curb or stop progress towards that change happening.

A person's neurobiological responses made sense at some point during their development and many of them will remain appropriate and relevant to the person throughout their life. But this is not always the case - some responses might have always been inappropriate due to being developed from a misrepresentation of a situation, and other responses will become less relevant in the process of growing up or as the environment changes. However, those initial neurobiological responses can be deeply-seated and predominately nonconscious, such that the person feels unable and unwilling to adapt or control them. Therefore, a current situation may trigger responses related to a previous negative experience, which in turn may create a less suitable reaction to the current situation. This can happen because the person is fused with their emotional response and reasons that "it must be true that this is unreasonable or scary to do, as I am feeling fearful". For example, a young child has a traumatic incident involving their grandfather. Later in their successful career, they wonder why they are always so anxious when meeting older male customers.

Neurobiological response: Self-preservation responses are strongly learned and have robust and quick-to-act neurobiological patterns, which tend towards the stance of *better safe than sorry*. They are strongly and persistently *felt* and *realised* to ensure that action is taken to escape the threat or to avoid getting closer to it. Physical responses, such as anxiety, fear, anger or nervousness, may occur and are intended to curb or stop any further *risky* actions. Thus the response may seem inappropriate to the situation, although the brain is purely operating given its current neurobiological patterns and inputs, which are significantly shaped by early life experiences.

People usually understand that they have a perception of a situation that affects how they view and react to it. The more comfortable someone feels about the consequences of changing, the more they tend to embrace acting differently. But the inner wish not to change becomes more compelling the more they perceive that the situation might actually be threatening to them. Threatening can be an actual threat (physical or perceived) and it can also be when someone strays too far from what is perceived as enabling them to survive and thrive – straying from what is *known to work*. Therefore, they view making that change to their behaviour as too risky and are more likely to decide that they responded appropriately with their existing behaviour. What people are often unaware of however is where this belief emanates from and why those responses are as they are.

And what can change that?

Facilitating a way forward: Responses sometimes feel unquestionably obvious and pertinent, which makes it harder to step aside from those responses and think about how to change them. However, understanding a little bit about the limitations of the brain and how it tends to operate and why, can enable a coachee to take a more detached perspective. This can open up possibilities and enable coachees to progress their coaching goals and change their behaviour. The new perspective often facilitates a conversation about handling reflexive hindering as and when it happens, as well as how to work through it in milder forms. The coachee can also experiment more easily with different actions towards their outcomes by learning to expect and manage reflexive hindering as it occurs.

Overall, there are three main considerations, informed by my research and coaching experience, that have driven the development of this book. They can basically be summed up as: *It would be good to know what you are up against.*

1. Coaching seeks to explore the situation, what helps and what hinders. I believe it is also worth exploring some aspects of the brain when reflexive-hindering is present. Coachees can then appreciate what they are *up against* with respect to themselves and can make more informed choices.

2. Point 1 creates a firmer basis for believing that change can happen as these aspects of *who someone is* are not as absolute as they feel. It appears helpful to appreciate that this seemingly innate response is probably a learned response where the person was not fully aware of that happening.

3. It is useful to think about, at a high level, what it realistically might take to achieve some of these changes.

Knowing this information about the brain in a rational, matter-of-fact way can be insightful for the coachee in understanding how they may hamper their own progress. It can explain the seemingly contradictory responses and thoughts that might be present. This new awareness often gives a coachee a different perspective and the ability to explore a greater variety of actions during coaching.

Be realistic about your brain

It is awesome | **It has limitations**

- Hundreds of types of neurons, neurochemicals and other cells
- In 1mm³, approx. 1bil connection sites, tens of 1000s of neurons & 4km of connecting tissue
- Relatively integrated rather than separately functioning areas

- The brain seeks to repeat what gets rewarded/ to avoid or reduce threat
- Same basic structure as each other & individually modified by experience

- Neurons are like factories: taking in, using, converting, generating and releasing different things
- Humans are a complex system – responses have different probabilities but every action is you

"Just doing" — managing allostasis

- It's busy inside
- Not an unquestionable truth
- Assumes and Approximates
- Evolved not designed
- Like a vibrant city
- More or less developed by 25

- It's not all-encompassing: illusionists make the most of this
- *Seeing & hearing* happen in the brain not in the eyes & ears

- Improves reaction times and conserves energy
- Predicts what is being sensed and updates the difference

- Advantageous aspects survive better
- Evolution takes time, so we are making the best of what we have

Be realistic about your brain

It is awesome

- Hundreds of types of neurons, neurochemicals and other cells
- In 1mm³, approx. 1bil connection sites, tens of 1000s of neurons & 4km of connecting tissue
- Relatively integrated rather than separately functioning areas

It's busy inside

The brain is awesome and limited. It does not have the capability to take in everything that is happening at any given moment, construct that present reality, and respond to it unaffected by previous experiences. It is a biological system and employs various techniques to appear to seamlessly and coherently navigate life. The brain also adapts amazingly well to some significant adversities and copes with a neurobiological structure which has evolved rather than being purpose-designed for modern human life.

The brain looks relatively static but there is a lot going on inside. In 1mm³ there are an estimated 1 billion connection sites, tens of 1000s of neurons and 4km of connecting tissue. The brain has 85-150 billion neurons and many more (maybe up to 50 times more) other cells, all working together. Neuroscientists are not certain about these figures, so not everything regarding neuroscience and the brain is a certain as it may appear – worth remembering. There are hundreds of types of neurons and glial cells, which often have thousands of connections and inputs. Whilst neurons are known to trigger (excite) other neurons to activate, they also inhibit other neurons from operating.

There are hundreds of chemicals enabling the brain to work. Some act within milli-seconds and some act over hours. Some flood the brain and others precisely target specific areas or receptors. They adjust various aspects of brain function, including the effectiveness of neural transmission and how quickly or slowly neurochemicals are absorbed.

The brain is not as compartmentalised as is often portrayed because neurons form networks and as Seeburger (2024) explains, "Your brain is dynamic. Nothing is just on or off.". It appears that most neurons connect to local neighbours, with far fewer connecting across the brain. The longer connections are very fast, otherwise they would take too long to create reactions. Together neurons create filters, amplify and/ or invert signals, and inhibit other pathways. Inputs tend to be initially processed at a basic level and then more complex integration (and interpretation) takes place as those signals progress through the neural pathways.

It is awesome

Be realistic about your brain

People are usually born with basically the same brain structure and on a large scale most brains look very similar. At birth there are an excess of neurons, which means there are enough pathway options to accommodate all the different experiences of different people.

Pathways are formed and honed from every experience – from the inputs at that time and the outcomes that happen. This allows the brain to form the necessary and personalised pathways so that each person can navigate the unique life they have been experiencing. Most of the unused neurons are pruned out before the teenage years.

Brains are strongly modified through experience up until approximately 25 years old as the brain is still developing up to that point. During those years a person has many experiences. If a response is positive the brain reinforces doing more of it and if it was painful/ threatening, then the brain reinforces minimising or avoiding it.

From around 25yrs onwards, the brain is relatively stable and the pathways, or *habits*, are then used repeatedly throughout someone's life. Most of a person's neural pathways (their habits) are therefore developed in the formative years without people realizing it. Consequently, people have not explicitly chosen the brain they have, nor many of the ways they interpret life.

However, subtle changes to the neural pathways are happening all the time as every moment and every experience finely hones their neural connections. New *habits* can therefore be proactively developed by consciously practicing new behaviours and having new experiences, which in turn, subtly change the neural pathways.

- The brain seeks to repeat what gets rewarded/ to avoid or reduce threat
- Same basic structure as each other & individually modified by experience

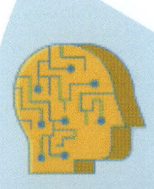

More or less developed by 25

It is awesome

Be realistic about your brain

The brain is a biological system and I liken it to a vibrant city – with elements moving around, being used, processed and created, or being passed from one neuron to thousands of others. All so someone can go about their daily life.

Using the city analogy to reflect on the brain: From a distance a city looks fairly static (as does the brain), although there is a lot of traffic and lots of people walking around. There are also buildings that look inactive, although inside they are busy as well. Now imagine that there is a sudden downpour of rain (akin to neurochemicals being released in the brain). The city responds in many different ways depending on the rain's impact: plants may flourish, although people may rush into nearby shops. Flash flooding can cause road closures in one area and traffic jams elsewhere due to re-routed traffic. The brain is like this vibrant city, with lots going on as well. Each neuron is like a factory taking in items, using them, manufacturing others, transporting them out and tidying up. Neurochemicals (like the rain) speed things up, slow things down, enhance some parts and shut down others.

Magnesium, calcium, potassium and sodium are important in the brain. They flow in and out of neurons, changing a neuron's negative or positive charge, which in turn creates neural activation or inhibition. Neurons are bathed in hundreds of neurochemicals, not just the five or six that tend to dominate some literature. Judith Glaser talks about the need for a "healthy neurochemical cocktail" in her book 'Conversational Intelligence'. This is a great analogy to remember and a good question to ask is, "how is my neurochemical cocktail at this moment?"

Brains are complex systems. When someone says "that wasn't like me", effectively it is them but in an unusual set of circumstances. It is a behaviour that has a low probability of happening, although when certain conditions arise then it becomes the one that the neural pathways activate. Perhaps the responses with the highest probability of happening are what someone recognises as *who they are*.

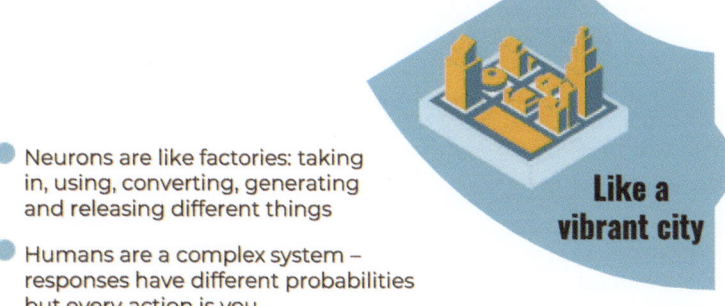

Like a vibrant city

- Neurons are like factories: taking in, using, converting, generating and releasing different things
- Humans are a complex system – responses have different probabilities but every action is you

Be realistic about your brain

It has limitations

It can be useful to know that the brain has evolved and is often using neurobiological aspects which have existed for a long time, rather than what might have been created if it was designed from scratch. Some of these work well for us and others less so. For example:

- The bones in your ear evolved from the reptilian jawbone. Some reptiles use these bones within their jaw to pick up vibrations from animals, enabling the reptile to locate its prey. For humans, these bones have migrated backwards into the ears and their vibration-detecting ability is used to detect sound (air vibrations).
- 50,000 years ago stressors were different, although the brain's threat response system appears not to have changed much since then. However, modern life has dramatically changed, especially regarding stressors, which are more prevalent nowadays and more removed from being an actual threat to life.

This *evolved not designed* aspect can lead to responses that are not necessarily the most effective at that moment, for that particular situation.

Generally, advantageous adaptations tend to become more prevalent as they usually enhance the ability to survive and thrive. Over time they can became a dominant feature. For example, tri-colour vision is advantageous for seeing potential predators and food (such as ripe fruit). This adaptation has therefore become the prevalent vision system for humans, along with a large percentage of the brain allocated to visual processing. Other animals are different and have their specific adaptations. For example, a dog has 220 million smell receptors, whereas, humans have only 5-6 million.

It can be easy to personify and caricature the brain. For example, the brain is neither *deciding* nor *competing with itself*, in the sense that these statements can imply. It does not *get things wrong* nor *make the right decision*, per se. Without being reductionist, it can be useful to remember that it is a biological system, albeit an awesome one.

Evolved not designed

● Advantageous aspects survive better

● Evolution takes time, so we are making the best of what we have

Be realistic about your brain

It has limitations

One aspect that makes the brain look awesome and seamless, is that it makes assumptions and uses approximations. This saves on energy and improves reaction times. For example, to catch a ball, the brain approximates where to put the hand given what the eyes are seeing. Then it checks what happened and adjusts accordingly. Otherwise, reaction times would be too slow.

The brain cannot store a 100% real-time version of everything it is sensing as it has neither the capacity nor resources to do that. Thus, most of what is thought to be seen in real-time is a prediction that is updated with inputs from the visual senses.

Anil Seth says we are "prediction machines", in that we are predicting the future based on the past. His talk has some good examples of this, both visually and auditorily (resources section, page 45).

Some of these assumptions, although well-embedded, have become outdated. For instance, the Scientific American article 'Seeing is believing' gives a good example. It illustrates that the brain tends to assume that there is only one light source – the sun. Nowadays however we have many more light sources than this.

Assumes and Approximates

- Improves reaction times and conserves energy
- Predicts what is being sensed and updates the difference

It appears that the brain works *top-down* (cortex) and *bottom-up* (sensory inputs). Sometimes the *top* predicts and checks out that prediction from the *bottom* (gains inputs to verify or dispute the prediction). Sometimes an input from the *bottom* will provoke a reaction from the *top* (typically an urgent corrective reaction).

Cortex (*top*)		Sensory inputs (*bottom*)
predicts	→	checks
use/ignore	←	input

Be realistic about your brain

It has limitations

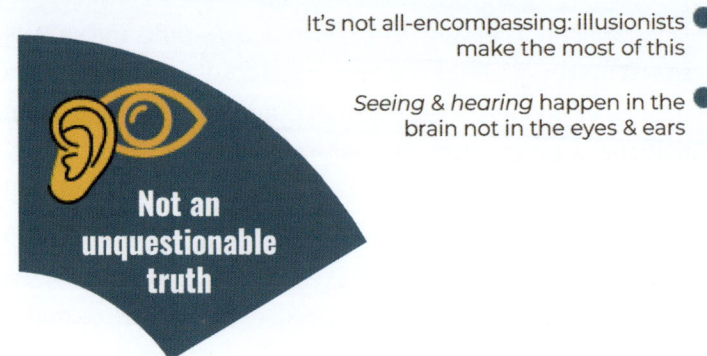

- It's not all-encompassing: illusionists make the most of this
- *Seeing & hearing* happen in the brain not in the eyes & ears

Not an unquestionable truth

The brain is a complex biological system with limited resources, adapted for human survival. As a result, what people believe they are sensing is not an *unquestionable truth*.

- A short video called the 'Colour Changing Card Trick' is a good demonstration of some of the hidden ways that the brain operates. The short talk by Dr Ramachandran demonstrates other insightful aspects.

- Examples demonstrating how we *see* with our brain rather than with our eyes include, how the blood vessels in front of the eye's lens are not seen, nor the blurred image when the eyes move. The brain smoothes these issues out and creates a clear image of what is important for surviving and thriving. The same is true for hearing, therefore, what is heard is not always the sound or speech that happened.

- Strange things can also happen due to the brain's complexity and biological nature. Synaesthesia is a condition where people have their senses cross-wired. For example, when they see a colour, they also get a particular taste in their mouth; or when they hear a sound, they see a particular colour. It is quite a different world for these people and is more common than might be expected.

- Mistakes also happen. Sometimes parts of the brain do not develop fully or as expected. For example, people born with only one or an under-developed brain hemisphere can lead relatively normal lives as the other hemisphere can compensate to some extent.

- The brain hates discrepancies so it tends to create reasonable (to the person) scenarios to explain them. It is commonly called post-rationalisation, although it can be more severe. For example, people with paralysed limbs may repeatedly state that they are choosing not to move the limb, but could if they wanted to.

| How can this happen? | **Our responses are influenced by our past experiences and our neurobiology** | What happens? |

Developed to ensure you survive and thrive

Early memories and traumatic events ...

... can feel *real* when triggered

Habits conserve energy: life is a series of habits.

"Better safe than sorry" approach to threat

Brains are complex wet-systems so,

irrelevant inputs can get linked to major events

Memories get altered over time,

and can be triggered by weak associations

All inputs go into our brain to varying degrees,

thus we can react to nonconscious stimuli

Humans have expanded the definition of threat ...

to social threats such as humiliation and "likes"

Safe & Threat responses
Stephen Porges

Safe mode
Curious, compassionate, connected to others
Able to problem solve, be creative
Inhibited threat response, smiling

Socially Engage

Fight / Flight mode
Aggressive, frustration, anxiety, fear
Reduced thinking & immune system
Sensitive to threats
Motionless face

Mobilise

Freeze mode
Overwhelm, helplessness, feeling trapped
Withdrawn, *robot like* – do as told
Reduced social awareness

Immobilise

How can this happen? Our responses are influenced by our past experiences and our neurobiology

Developed to ensure you survive and thrive

Early memories and traumatic events ...
... can feel *real* when triggered

Habits conserve energy: life is a series of habits.
"Better safe than sorry" approach to threat

People's responses have been useful at some point - many still are, many have changed and some have become outdated. The latter appear more resistant to changing when circumstances change, thus creating responses not entirely appropriate to the situation being faced. This is someone's neurobiology striving to keep them safe, albeit with pathways strongly influenced by their formative years. Therefore, it is useful if the person can be generous to themselves when reflexive hindering happens, as this response was beneficial to them in some way, at some point.

Experiences can be quite impactful during someone's early years as they have less reasoning ability and fewer experiences to help temper their emotions and perceptions of a situation. Early powerfully emotional experiences therefore create strong pathways and connections that become disproportionately influential. If at a later time, a situation triggers a pathway leading to one of those memories, it can strongly affect someone's thinking and behaviour in that instance.

Traumatic events are stored as implicit memories* so they are not recognised as *being remembered* and they can be quite real for the person when triggered, as if happening for them at that moment. The brain dislikes discrepancies and rationalises the experience. For example, "I can hear a loud explosion, it's not a memory I've recalled, therefore it has to be actually happening for real, now" and for the person the explosion is *real* and *happening* at that moment. (Remember *seeing* and *hearing* happen inside the brain.) Explicit memories* do not develop until after 2/3 years old. Before this age experiences also tend to be stored as implicit memories and therefore appear innate.

The brain makes things as automatic as possible to conserve energy. Once a response becomes a habit, this frees up the conscious working memory for important things that require attention, meaning habits make life work. Sometimes however habits are created to avoid a dreaded outcome and are rarely rechecked to see if they are still relevant. That habit might have been formed during someone's early years, but now that they are much older they probably have different capabilities to handle it. However, an avoidance habit nudges people away from venturing to find out if the situation still needs to be avoided or if a different approach would be better.

* Implicit memory is unconscious recall, like riding a bike. Explicit memory is conscious recall, such as recalling a holiday memory.

| How can this happen? | **Our responses are influenced by our past experiences and our neurobiology** |

Developed to ensure you survive and thrive

People tend to think that all responses are just about the immediate situation. However, the brain is a wet system and it is not as discrete in its pathway generation as might be assumed. Other non-related experiences, which happened at the same time as the stressful event, can become linked to that event as well. So when someone has that non-related experience again and it inadvertently triggers the pathway linked to the stressful memory, they might behave in an unexpected way. A negative response could therefore be caused by something about another person or the environment that is related to an old experience. The negative response is not truly about the current situation, although people are often not aware of what it is actually about. For example, music played at a sad occasion (e.g. a funeral) when heard elsewhere can cause a person to cry, although they may not remember that association.

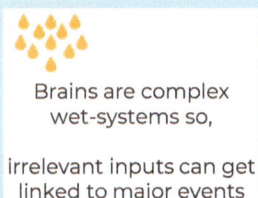

Brains are complex wet-systems so,

irrelevant inputs can get linked to major events

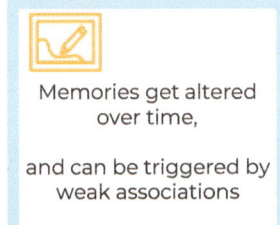

Memories get altered over time,

and can be triggered by weak associations

Memories are not as sound as they are often portrayed and are not accurate recreations of whatever it was - unlike photographs in an album. Pathways and connections change when memories are retrieved and when they are re-stored. This means people often have different recollections from what really happened. It seems that memories are stored more like a recipe, and potentially across the whole brain. So when an input occurs, it triggers a *recipe* to recreate the memory. However, akin to using other recipes, the recreated memory is never quite the same each time. This is because when a memory is accessed people are in a different state to when it happened and there are different neurochemicals present, at different concentrations than before. Talking about a memory with others also changes that memory and it is that subtly updated version that is re-stored.

It appears that some new neurons are created within the memory area, although the current perspective is that new neurons are not created elsewhere post-25yrs old. The brain only has so many neurons and consequently some get repurposed. This means that neural memory connections become altered, get used elsewhere or are overlaid as new memories are made. Over time, memories can become less accurate and, as memories inform our perception of things, these changes can unknowingly affect how we respond in a situation.

How can this happen? Our responses are influenced by our past experiences and our neurobiology

Developed to ensure you survive and thrive

Sometimes people respond in the way they do due to the nonconscious processing of sensory inputs. This happens because all sensory inputs enter the brain and activate nonconscious low-level processing to some extent. Most of this activity fades away, although sometimes it triggers higher level processing and this may or may not become conscious depending on the nature of the response. Blindsight is a good example of how the brain can process visual inputs outside of conscious awareness (resources section, page 46). Hearing your name spoken at a party is an example of when the inputs trigger a conscious response. A person at a party can be very focused on what their friend is saying and the rest is just background noise, until someone else mentions their name. It is amazing how the person suddenly hears that and can switch their attention to the other conversation to check out the thought, "what is that about?"

This can happen with feelings as well. They are evoked and become consciously felt, although what triggered the feeling remains outside of conscious awareness. The feeling gets linked to the situation at that moment, as the brain dislikes discrepancies. This affects thoughts and behaviour as the person's rationale becomes, "I'm talking to these people and I'm feeling anxious. It must be something about them, therefore I should be extra cautious".

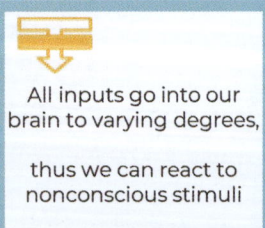

All inputs go into our brain to varying degrees, thus we can react to nonconscious stimuli

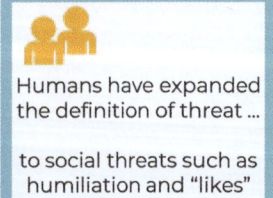

Humans have expanded the definition of threat ... to social threats such as humiliation and "likes"

The threat response developed when threats were more closely linked to survival and it has not really evolved for modern life. Uncertainty, strangers and movement all trigger a level of threat response. These happen more frequently in modern life, so the threat response is stimulated more often, increasing anxiety and vigilance. People also worry about being excluded or disadvantaged as survival often relies on others. 50,000 years ago it was very important to be included in the tribe, so perceptions matter. In today's larger and global communities there are more ways for this social threat to arise or be perceived. This leads to more frequent triggering of the threat response, resulting in some reactions being disproportionate to the threat. The long-term biological effects of this can be detrimental to health.

Our responses are influenced by our past experiences and our neurobiology

What happens?

The Polyvagal Theory*, by Stephen Porges, describes three basic responses by the autonomic nervous system to situations and their associated threat level. Porges named the responses: Social Engagement (*safe*) mode, Mobilisation (*fight/ flight*) mode and Immobilisation (*freeze*) mode. He suggests that the level of risk perceived in the environment is nonconscious and that the responses are spontaneous and involuntary.

The parasympathetic nervous system (associated with a calmer, rhythmic heart rate) drives the Social Engagement mode and also part of it drives the Immobilisation mode. The sympathetic nervous system (associated with a faster heart rate) drives the Mobilisation mode.

When the brain perceives the environment to be safe, the Social Engagement mode enables interaction with others and being more open to possibilities. When the brain perceives the environment as threatening, then biological changes prepare the body for mobilisation – either to fight the threat or to flee from it.

If the situation is perceived as inescapable and a threat to actual survival, the brain triggers the third response: Immobilisation. Immobilisation is, in essence, about feigning death, which frequently results in a predator losing interest. It may also take the form of shutting down the body to cope with overwhelm.

The above aspects are likely to play a role in reflexive hindering, especially if it intensifies.

* Porges, S. W. (2011). *The polyvagal theory: Neurophysiological foundations of emotions, attachment, communication, and self-regulation (Norton series on interpersonal neurobiology)*. WW Norton & Company.

Our responses are influenced by our past experiences and our neurobiology

What happens?

When the brain perceives a situation to be safe, the Social Engagement mode enables curiosity, exploration and interaction with others. There is also a "healthy neurochemical cocktail"* in the brain. This mode lightens facial expressions, improves the immune system's operation, and is the easiest state for learning and thinking to take place.

Safe mode characteristics:
- Curious, compassionate, joyful, generous, mindful, connected to others
- Facially expressive, vocal intonation, eye contact
- Calm heart rate, although can become energised
- Immune system boosted and good circulation
- Inhibited threat response

> **Safe mode**
> Curious, compassionate, connected to others
> Able to problem solve, be creative
> Inhibited threat response, smiling
>
> *Socially Engage*

The parasympathetic nervous system is active in this mode and the heart rate is lower and more rhythmic. The immune system functions as it would under normal circumstances. Blood flows throughout the brain, allowing neurochemicals, other substances (oxygen, etc) to be moved to where they are required. This enables the brain to function more holistically.

The threat response is also suppressed, which means that it is actively inhibited rather than just turned down. For example, when sitting close to someone the threat response naturally triggers, but the threat response is inhibited when that person is deemed safe. This means re-evaluating what is perceived as safe. As a result, things generally seem more acceptable and people are able to be more open to possibilities. They are willing to explore riskier ideas and diverse options, leading to new actions. Consequently, it is more beneficial to think, reason, decide, etc in a calmer and less anxious state of mind.

In *Safe mode*, people are typically more facially expressive and have better eye contact. These signals say to people, "I am approachable, I am nice to be with, I am safe" and people therefore engage with them differently.

* Judith Glaser (2016) coined the term "healthy neurochemical cocktail" (Ref 28)

Our responses are influenced by our past experiences and our neurobiology

What happens?

When the brain perceives a situation as threatening, the sympathetic nervous system becomes active and biological changes prepare the body to fight or flee. Specific neurochemicals are released and blood is diverted to areas crucial for mobilisation. This can affect thoughts, mood and behaviour for up to 24hrs. If the response persists over the long-term, then memory-forming cells can wither and die. Overall, there are reductions in someone's ability to learn, think broadly, stay healthy, and be seen as approachable.

Fight / Flight mode characteristics:
- Aggressive, frustration, anxiety, fear
- Still face, voice pitch raised, minimal eye contact
- Increased heart rate, release of cortisol and adrenalin
- Blood pumped to key areas and withdrawn from others, reduced immune system
- Narrowed thinking, overly sensitive to threats

Fight / Flight mode
Aggressive, frustration, anxiety, fear
Reduced thinking & immune system
Sensitive to threats
Motionless face

Mobilise

This mode narrows people's focus, heightens their sense of threat (expands what is considered to be threatening), increases their threat vigilance and creates faster reactions to perceived threats. It increases blood pressure as well as suppressing the immune system and other biological aspects less involved in fighting or fleeing.

50,000+ years ago threats were less frequent than they are today, but were more likely to be life threatening. Therefore, the threat response can be quite powerful. Biologically many things happen, including the brain's threat-response networks receiving more oxygen and a reduction in oxygen elsewhere. Attention becomes fixed on the threat (*best to know where it is*) rather than rationalising and reasoning, which take more time. Facial effects include the face becoming motionless and reduced eye contact, both of which signal threat to others. This makes others, consciously or unconsciously, cautious about engaging with this person. The heart rate is increased to pump blood (oxygen) faster to body areas required for mobilisation. Fatty acids are also released to provide energy. These often get deposited along arteries causing them to narrow as, in most instances, there is no fighting or fleeing. This can cause longer-term problems as future threat responses will be pumping blood at higher pressure through narrower arteries.

Our responses are influenced by our past experiences and our neurobiology

What happens?

When the brain perceives the situation as inescapable (a perceived threat to actual survival), it triggers the third response: Immobilisation. The rationale is that feigning death in front of a predator often leads to the predator losing interest and going away. It can also be about shutting down the body to cope with overwhelm, in whatever form that is taking.

Freeze mode characteristics:
o Overwhelm, helplessness and feeling trapped
o Socially withdrawn and reduced social awareness
o Decreased heart rate and blood pressure
o Increased endorphins to reduce pain and numb experience
o Faint, light headed, inwardly focused

Shutting down is emulated in various ways and its severity depends on the situation and the person. For many it may simply mean withdrawing from a conversation, going silent, not caring or just doing the minimum in a robot-like manner. Others may disconnect from social interaction in some form and/ or feel hopelessness. Sometimes, if a person is very overwhelmed, then immobilisation can result in them blacking out. This is often associated with burn-out.

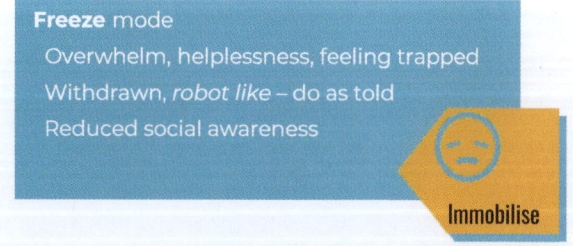

Freeze mode
Overwhelm, helplessness, feeling trapped
Withdrawn, *robot like* – do as told
Reduced social awareness

Immobilise

| Is it possible? | Change is possible and takes commitment | How could I do it? |

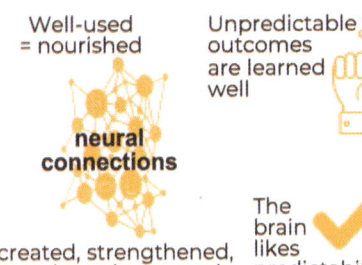

- constantly adapt

- to enhance learning & thinking

Neural pathways

New experiences

Use these insights to detach from reflexive hindering and reflect upon it

Create Safe mode

Refocused AtTention

- change pathways

- is a useful distraction method

31

Is it possible? Change is possible and takes commitment

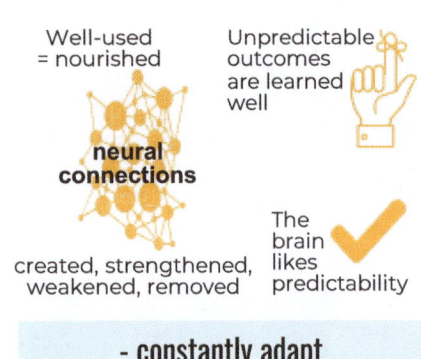

Popular literature on neuroplasticity seems to imply that it is limitless, although further reading shows that that does not appear to be the case. Dr Sarah McKay's article on 'Can you think yourself into a different person' soberingly lays out the reality - the brain is not plasticine and change takes effort. In reality, during adulthood, *neuroplasticity* often means *synaptic-plasticity*.

Synaptic connections are constantly changing, by their thousands, every second. During every moment connections are created, removed, strengthened and weakened. Well-used connections are also nourished and often expand in size. It is estimated that 20% of the brain's neural connections have changed every 24hrs. These minute alterations subtly change responses and it is these natural changes that can be utilised to create intentional change.

Unpredictable outcomes could mean uncertainty, reduced safety and may be life-threatening. Predictability means certainty, safety and less need for learning, which conserves valuable resources. The brain therefore loves predictability as it enhances survival.

The brain perceives unpredictable situations as potentially life-threatening so it needs to learn quickly and thoroughly in order to make them more predictable in the future. Therefore, when the brain predicts an outcome will be X but the outcome is Y, the mismatch (prediction error) creates enhanced learning, forming strong neural pathways. Thus significant learning happens from very unexpected outcomes as the brain acts to learn from the situation until its prediction matches the outcome.

A prediction error can however be caused by unexpected positive outcomes. These are often called an *aha moment*, a valuable insight, or a surprising result from a new behaviour. This means that positive, unexpected outcomes are also strongly reinforced and can accelerate beneficial change within someone.

Is it possible?

Change is possible and takes commitment

In *Social Engagement (Safe) mode* the parasympathetic nervous system is active. This improves the ability to think more broadly due to the threat response being suppressed. It is also easier to be more open and to explore possibly riskier ideas and options. Purposefully enhancing the ability to stay in or regain *Safe mode* is useful for combating reflexive hindering, as that creates a better chance of practicing and embedding new pathways.

Suggested ways for activating *Safe mode*:

- Being compassionate, generous or appreciative to yourself or others
- Showing gratitude towards others
- Mindfulness and meditation reduce stress and anxiety
- Authentically smiling and laughing
- Feeling proud, especially of someone else
- Learning self-compassion

If the parasympathetic system is activated, someone can have a very different conversation with themselves and others. It is more thoughtful about the situation and/ or the other person's point of view. Possible options on how to navigate or resolve the situation emerge more easily. There tends to be more acceptance of things rather than fixating on certain viewpoints and the issue.

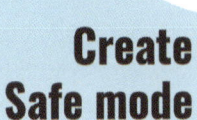

When practicing a new behaviour, the reflexive hindering response may initially intensify in an attempt to stop the old behaviour from being changed.

However, knowing about reflexive hindering gives an appreciation of these following aspects:

1) The response is not fully related to the situation being faced nor the *you* facing it
2) The intensified response can be tolerated in order to persevere with practicing the new behaviours
3) Giving the brain new experiences with positive outcomes will build additional capability to handle situations more appropriately in the future

For these reasons, the person needs to be appreciative of their efforts and keep practicing their new behaviours.

Change is possible and takes commitment

How could I do it?

Someone's current neural pathways have been honed by practice throughout life, even if they were not aware of it. Therefore, it is reasonable to believe that pathways can be adapted or established to create change. This takes effort and a realistic view of what is possible. Therefore, someone must think about what they genuinely are, and are not, going to do.

Inevitably, change requires committed practice and reflection. Most people learn a new skill through repeated practice and reflecting upon that (e.g. playing an instrument, a sport, driving). This means scheduling time for practice and reflection. It is recognized that new skills take practice to become good at them. Yet that same level of practice does not always seem to be applied to creating behaviour change, even though it is also about honing a new skill. Perhaps, people are less convinced that it will be worth the effort required.

New experiences - change pathways

Sometimes there is concern about the consequences of a change as it feels more fundamental than learning a new sport or musical instrument. Coaching can help in these situations by working through those concerns as well as enabling viable and sustainable practice to take place. It is useful to practice in the safe environment of the coaching session as people are most open to learning in safe environments. For example, practice a new way of doing something with the coach and work through how to navigate each step. Also, work through what obstacles might prevent practice from taking place and how to overcome them. Practice gives the brain a chance to experience different options, which strengthens weaker connections and/ or builds new neural pathways. This is especially true if a different option demonstrates that a person's concerns are either unfounded, or that they can be successfully mitigated or navigated.

Some experts once thought that painful memories could be extinguished but now that does not seem to be totally true. At best, it appears that stronger alternative pathways can be created, although in exceptional circumstances, the old pathway may still get triggered. However, someone should not be despondent nor give up if this occasionally happens. They need to keep going and be generous to themselves because the more the new pathways are strengthened, the more often they will be used instead.

Change is possible and takes commitment

How could I do it?

When a reflexive hindering response becomes intrusive, consciously switching attention can be helpful and often has the effect of changing how someone feels as well. For example: someone is feeling annoyed about something and their child runs in, laughing and smiling, to tell them some wonderful news. It is amazing how fast they can snap out of that negative feeling. This concept can be used with reflexive hindering. Minimising the effect of reflexive hindering is especially important if that enables someone to achieve a different and positive outcome.

Therefore, think about how to consciously change attention by switching and becoming fully absorbed in something else. It can be quite simple and often brings attention into the present moment, rather than inwardly ruminating or speculating. For example, NLP coaching uses the technique of getting people to recite their telephone number backwards to clear the mind between exercises as it is a quick and simple way of shifting attention. Purely thinking about needing to calm down or to stop worrying rarely works, as these are just thoughts rather than actions that actually calm someone down or stops them worrying.

Here are a few examples of simple actions that can be taken to refocus attention.

- Practical mindfulness - absorb yourself in what you are doing and notice how you are doing it, how it feels, what you are hearing and seeing. E.g., make a coffee/ tea, make lunch, wash your hands, walk outside and observe – see, hear, feel, smell.
- Ask a question about what you are doing and answer it – write down your answer.
- Engage in a positive/ joyful conversation.
- Read a book/ report/ article out loud: read a couple of sentences and then ask yourself, "what are the key points here?"
- Counting the number of different coloured cars whilst walking helps switch attention, as does manual arithmetic.

What other actions would also work?

Refocused AtTention

Focus on some details
Engage in an activity
Absorb yourself in something
Mindfully do something

- is a useful distraction method

Part 2 – MERE Coaching Conversations

A four-step process to support coaches using the infographic with their coachees

Mastering

Enabling

Realising

Practice
Embedding

Simple insights creating surprising shifts

> Coaches, "Embrace neuroscience and be a coach rather than a neuroscientist. Relax, engage your enthusiasm for where it could take your coachee and use neuroscience on your terms."

Ontological coaching advocates that a coach is well placed to help a coachee uncover how their experiences and perspectives on the world have shaped them. Counselling research proposes that neuroeducation shifts clients from passive bystanders to actively contributing. There is also practitioner coaching literature that states that it can sometimes be helpful for coaches and coachees to *think about thinking* and suggests that neuroscience is well suited for that. Other practitioner coaching literature suggests that some coachees may prefer a neuroscience-based, rather than conceptual, approach. The doctoral research underpinning this book supports these statements and demonstrated that the use of neuroeducation during a coaching session can be beneficial within the context of reflexive hindering.

The research showed the coaches felt that their coachees derived value from the infographic-based conversation. They felt their coachees gained three to five of these benefits:
- An explanatory understanding of brain function that makes pertinent aspects more evident (inc. a recognition as to what may be driving the reflexive hindering)
- Real insights that make a difference (inc. realising that the response has been learned and can be changed)
- Creating a subject to object shift (being able to objectively discuss the dynamic from a detached perspective)
- Increased motivation for taking action
- Having more self-compassion (and compassion for others) due to better acceptance of reflexive hindering and its underlying intent
- Enhancing hope or belief within the coachee that change can happen

The coaches also stated that they had gained from three to six of the benefits listed below, from using the infographic:
- Created an immersive and enlightening neuroscience-based exploration
- Enabled different conversations
- Was a useful structure and aide-memoir
- Can be an easy-to-use neuroscience-based tool
- Gave the coach a deeper understanding of neuroscience personally
- Gave the coach's neuroscience conversation credibility because the infographic is well-referenced and underpinned with factual data

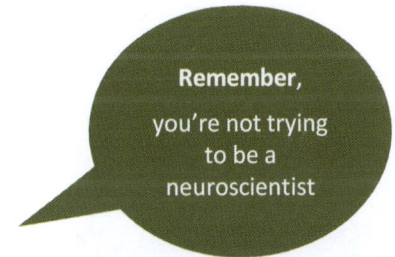

Remember, you're not trying to be a neuroscientist

The infographic conversation works well when the coach authentically connects it to the coachee and their goals. By making it relevant, the above benefits can be obtained even if the coach is selective about which elements are explored. The MERE Coaching Conversation steps have been designed to help the coach use the infographic in an embedded way so that it facilitates an exploration rather than an explanation. This helps the information to resonate with the coachee and provides insights on reflexive hindering that create shifts and enable the coachee to have new perspectives on their responses.

MERE Coaching Conversations
Simple insights creating surprising shifts

Mastering
- Learn about reflexive hindering
- Understand the infographic elements

Enabling
- Link use of infographic to coaching outcomes and/or reflexive hindering observed
- Have an immersive and exploratory discussion

Realising
- A real insight that makes a difference
- A more powerful belief/ hope that change can happen
- Increase in self-compassion and compassion for others
- Invigorated commitment to taking actions occurs

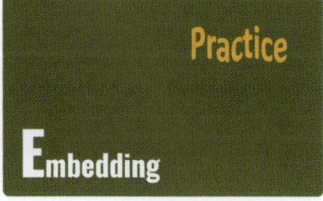
Practice
Embedding
- Agree robust actions and commitment to continued practice
- Build resolve to tolerate discomfort through the early stages of change

M - mastering

Mastering

- ❖ Learn about reflexive hindering
- ❖ Understand the infographic elements

What is this step about?

- ✓ Learn about reflexive hindering and how it impedes your coachee's progress.
- ✓ Understand the infographic's three high level messages and its story, as well as the role and detail of each element (see Part 1). Then practice and rehearse these with colleagues, family, etc.
- ✓ The above actions enable you to make informed choices about how to use the infographic pragmatically to meet the needs of your coachee.

Tips from other coaches

- Use the infographic with appropriate coachees (reflexive hindering 3+ on schematic, p13).
- Ensure you have enough time. If not, reduce the amount covered.
- Have the infographic material ready just in case it becomes appropriate to use it.
- If you are using the paperback version, bring that out with your other coaching materials at the start of the meeting. This makes it easier to segway into using it.
- Tailor where you start on the infographic, and what you cover, to the coachee's needs. Be comfortable with what you leave out (knowing the infographic's flow helps you do this).
- Although preparation helps, a lot of preparation is not necessarily needed as you can use pages 12-35 alongside the infographic sections on pages 4-11.

E - enabling

- ❖ Link use of infographic to coaching outcomes and/or reflexive hindering observed
- ❖ Have an immersive and exploratory discussion

What is this step about?

- ✓ Allow the coachee to talk and bring the infographic in at an appropriate point.
- ✓ Demonstrate your authenticity for using the infographic and embed it into the coachee's outcomes and/ or observed reflexive hindering.

Tips from other coaches

- Take time in the coaching session to connect with the coachee and their coaching goals, so that you know how the infographic connects to the coachee's reflexive hindering and their coaching outcomes.
- Listen to the coachee's story and then weave that into positioning the infographic.
- Wait for an appropriate point to use the infographic so that the connection is stronger.
- Ask the coachee for permission to use the infographic, as you would with any other intervention.
- Put effort into demonstrating that you have thought about how sharing the infographic will be valuable for them and explicitly state that. Your conviction makes the conversation deeper than *just a lesson on the brain* as it becomes more real for the coachee because it is tailored to their situation. Consequently, they can see how it applies to them and, importantly, how they can apply it.

E - enabling

- ❖ Link use of infographic to coaching outcomes and/or reflexive hindering observed
- ❖ Have an immersive and exploratory discussion

What is this step about?

- ✓ Have an interactive discussion that creates an immersive and informative neurobiological exploration of their reflexive hindering.
- ✓ Have an explanatory conversation that makes it real for the coachee and normalises their reflexive hindering – make it more than just neuroeducation.

Tips from other coaches

- Enter into the world of the coachee's brain and explore it in the context of their coaching goal and reflexive hindering. Be deeply curious about the coachee and how their experience has shaped their interpretation of the world.
- Create curiosity –> to create insight –> to help the coachee become more objective.
- Deep-dive into the coachee's world when something resonates, leaving the infographic behind until it is appropriate to reconnect to it.
- Pause and invite observations. For example, describe some elements and then ask for observations. You could also allow your coachee to read an infographic section for themselves and then ask for their thoughts on what they have read.
- Use associated illustrative examples or analogies - use your own or draw from the immediate environment. Using personal examples demonstrates your own vulnerability and learning, which often enables the coachee to do the same.
- During the conversation, robustly connect the infographic information and illustrative examples to the coachee's reflexive-hindering experience. (Share the fact -> Bring it alive with an example -> Make it real by getting the coachee to give a personal example.)

R - realising

- A real insight that makes a difference
- A more powerful belief/ hope that change can happen
- Increase in self-compassion and compassion for others
- Invigorated commitment to taking actions occurs

What is this step about?

- ✓ A real insight that makes a difference to the coachee's understanding.
- ✓ A subject to object shift:
  - Coachee becomes objective towards reflexive hindering.
  - Coachee takes a more detached perspective on the situation regarding the brain's involvement.
- ✓ It creates a more powerful belief/ hope:
  - that change can happen
  - that the coachee can do something which is in their control to create that change
- ✓ Increase in self-compassion, by realising this is a neurobiological response rather than *something I am doing wrong*.
- ✓ Actions become more plausible and typically there is an invigorated commitment to taking actions.

Tips from other coaches

- The above points outline things that indicate a shift in perspective and a receptiveness to new possibilities by the coachee. These can enable the coachee to progress their coaching outcomes further.

E - embedding

Embedding / Practice

- ❖ Agree robust actions and commitment to continued practice
- ❖ Build resolve to tolerate discomfort through the early stages of change

What is this step about?

- ✓ The infographic conversation can:
    - reinforce what needs to happen to make the change sustainable.
    - emphasise the importance of continued practice .
- ✓ Agree robust actions and ensure their neurobiological benefits are reinforced.
- ✓ Revisit the infographic for strategies if reflexive hindering increases when the coachee first starts to experiment with new behaviours.
- ✓ Normalise any increase in reflexive hindering and build resolve to tolerate discomfort through the early stages of change.

Tips from other coaches

- Use your coaching experience to thoroughly work though the above points, as the embedding step is just as important as the other steps.
- Refer back to the infographic to reinforce commitment or gain clarification if required.
- Be very realistic and pragmatic at this point, as change happens through committed practice.
- Setbacks need to be discussed and reframed. The old pathways are not erased, although new ones can become much stronger and easier to use. Therefore, there will be situations in which the old habits reoccur – this is not a failure of the coachee, it is life. The coachee needs to be compassionate towards themselves and re-establish practicing their agreed actions as soon as they can.

References & other resources

Good books for an overview on the brain and the field of neuroscience:
Pinker, S. (2015). *How the mind works*. Penguin.
Barrett, L.F. (2020). *Seven and a half lessons about the brain*. Houghton Mifflin Harcourt.
Rose, N.S. & Abi-Rached, J.M. (2013). *Neuro: the new brain sciences and the management of the mind.* Princeton University Press.
Dingman, M. (2019). *Your brain, explained: what neuroscience reveals about your brain and its quirks*. Nicholas Brealey.

Other resources:
'The Brian': Six-part series of one-hour programmes by David Eagleman.
'The New Scientific Understanding of Emotions': A 90-min webinar by the IOC and Lisa Feldman-Barrett.
'How the brain works' from the University of London Centre for Educational Neuroscience.
'2-minute neuroscience: A neuroscience topic described in 2 minutes or less': Videos on a diversity of neuroscience items.
Jarrett, C. (2014). *Great myths of the brain*. John Wiley & Sons.
Hickok, G. (2014). *The Myth of Mirror Neurons.* W.W. Norton & Company Ltd.
Damasio, A.R. (2000). *The feeling of what happens: body and emotion in the making of consciousness.* Vintage.
Anglia Ruskin University - The neuroscience of self: how the brain creates 'me' (21 Mar 2014): A talk by Dr Jane Aspell, video.
Website: Dr Sarah McKay – many informative articles.
Website: The Neuroscience School (Dr Irena O'Brien) – many informative articles.

References for Reflexive Hindering (pages 12-15):

<u>Main reference, in particular Chapter 2, section 2.10</u>
Lyall, D. (2021). *Enhancing the efficacy of coaching: defining and exploring reflexive hindering using an applied neuroscience approach and a developed infographic.* Doctoral thesis, University of Wales Trinity St David Research Repository. https://repository.uwtsd.ac.uk/id/eprint/2442

<u>Supplementary references</u>
Gilbert, P. (2013). *The compassionate mind: a new approach to life's challenges*. Robinson.
Gilbert, P. (2014). The origins and nature of compassion focused therapy. *British Journal of Clinical Psychology*, 53(1), 6-41.
Kegan, R. & Lahey, L. (2009*). Immunity to change: how to overcome it and unlock the potential in yourself and your organization.* Harvard Business Press.
LeDoux, J. (2016). *Anxious: Using the Brain to Understand and Treat Fear and Anxiety*. Penguin.
Lyall, D., & Fillery-Travis, A. (2023). Improving the efficacy of coaching: Outlining reflexive hindering. *International Journal of Coaching Psychology*, 4(2), 1-18. https://ijcp.nationalwellbeingservice.com/volumes/volume-4-2023/volume-4-article-2/
Shabi, A., & Whybrow, A. (2019). Ontological coaching. In S. Palmer & A. Whybrow (Eds.), *Handbook of coaching psychology: A guide for practitioners* (2nd ed., pp. 219-228). Routledge.

References for page 17

* Ref no.	Where to find it in the reference text
1	p243-244, p250
5	p46, p147, p131-2, p148, chapter 2
7	p24
13	p 1926-1929
15	p53
16	p19, p63
17	chapter 2
19	p26, p179 -180
21	p41, p50, p58
25	P45-46
28	p29
32	p2380-2393
34	p49, p52, p56-60
35	p170
36	p8, p17, p22, p25, p114, p370-1, chapter 2 & 3 summaries, Sec 4.14-20, sec 4.7, Sec 3.11
39	p5, p15-18
41	p10, p16
47	P97
51	p16, p36, p108
52	p43-47, p175

Seeburger quote: 'How Brain Networks Sustain Attention' (Apr 12, 2024) https://neurosciencenews.com/attention-network-brain-25915/

Extra resources

'The Brian': Six-part series of one-hour programmes by David Eagleman.

'The New Scientific Understanding of Emotions': A 90-min webinar by the IOC and Lisa Feldman-Barrett.

'How the brain works' from the University of London Centre for Educational Neuroscience.

References for page 18

* Ref no.	Where to find it in the reference text
1	p279
4	p283
11	P43, p156
17	p127, chapter 7
21	p12
34	p3, p72
36	p191, p321, p546, Sec 7.1-7.2, Sec 7.13, Sec 10.14 summary
41	p10-11
51	p38

References for page 20

* Ref no.	Where to find it in the reference text
1	p278
14	p11
23	p1
25	P18
36	p133
42	p156-157, p165-174, p170, p213
47	p190
51	p98
61	Article

Extra resources

LeDoux, J. (2020).*The deep history of ourselves: The four-billion-year story of how we got conscious brains*. Penguin.

Cesario, J., Johnson, D.J. & Eisthen, H. (2019). Your Brain Is Not an Onion with a Tiny Reptile Inside, *Current Directions in Psychological Science*, 29(3), 255-260.

* Ref no. See pages 47-49 for the list of references this number relates to. For example, Ref no. 1 is reference 1 on page 47 (*Amthor, F. (2016). Neuroscience For Dummies (2nd ed.). John Wiley and Sons, Inc.*)

References for page 19

* Ref no.	Where to find it in the reference text
4	p284
7	chapter 2
31	throughout
34	p2
36	p65 summary, Sec 2.1-2.5, Sec 3.7-3.9

Extra resources

'The Brian': Six-part series of one-hour programmes by David Eagleman.

'The New Scientific Understanding of Emotions': A 90-min webinar by the IOC and Lisa Feldman-Barrett.

'How the brain works' from the University of London Centre for Educational Neuroscience.

References for page 21

* Ref no.	Where to find it in the reference text
1	p106, p169, p235
4	p27
19	p65, p75
21	p52-3, p56, chap 2
34	p182
42	p28-30
47	p53-54
60	P75

Extra resources

'How your eyes trick your mind' article by Melissa Hogenboom (2015, BBC Future)

'Seeing is believing' article by Scientific American (2008)

'Your brain hallucinates your conscious reality' by Anil Seth (2017, Ted Talk)

Seth, A. (2021). *Being you: A new science of consciousness*. Penguin.

Clark, A. (2015). *Surfing uncertainty: Prediction, action, and the embodied mind*. Oxford University Press.

References for page 22	
* Ref no.	Where to find it in the reference text
1	p80, p87, p235, p346
19	p30-37, chapter 1
20	p155, p258
22	paper
25	p17-20, p28, p45
27	article
34	p49
35	p34, p165
36	p20, p163, p272, Chaps 4 & 6
37	throughout
38	article
42	p29, p139, p387
47	p5-8, p45, p63-4, p68-71, p255-258, p266, p271, p281-2, chapter 3
51	p100, p102, p106, p112, p120
57	p52-54, p168, p269
60	p41-44

Extra resources

'Our Brains Predict Every Sound We Hear', Technology Networks, Neuroscience news & research (11 Jan, 2021)

'Seven strange quirks of human vision' by Emma Young, BPS (05 Mar, 2020)

'Colour changing card trick': Video with Richard Wiseman

'3 clues to understanding your brain' by VS Ramachandran (2007)

'What Is Synesthesia?' by Alina Bradford (October 18, 2017)

* Ref no. See pages 47-49 for the list of references this number relates to. For example, Ref no. 1 is reference 1 on page 47 (*Amthor, F. (2016). Neuroscience For Dummies (*2nd ed.). *John Wiley and Sons, Inc.)*

References for page 24	
* Ref no.	Where to find it in the reference text
11	p18-20
16	p79-81, p88-89
20	p75
25	p39-40, p152-153
34	p221
35	p75, p110
39	p129-131
40	article
53	article
54	p155-156
60	p75

References for section page 26	
* Ref no.	Where to find it in the reference text
1	p235, p274
19	p56, p59, p73-75
25	p39
35	p165, p205
47	p63-64
51	P100

Extra resources

'Blindsight the strangest form of consciousness' article by David Robson (2015, BBC Future)

Breuning, L.G. (2019). *Tame your anxiety: Rewiring your brain for happiness*. Rowman & Littlefield.

References for page 25	
* Ref no.	Where to find it in the reference text
7	p857-859
14	p57
21	p21-26
34	p97, p124, p135-136, p177
35	p182
39	p41-44
59	Article
60	book chapter

Extra resources

'False memories of crime appear real when retold to others' (8 Apr 2020), UCL News

Seth, A. (2021). *Being you: A new science of consciousness*. Penguin.

Eagleman, D. (2020). *Livewired: The inside story of the ever-changing brain*. Canongate Books.

References for pages 27-30	
* Ref no.	Where to find it in the reference text
1	p195
41	chap 9
43	p19-24
44	p116-144
45	Throughout
46	episode 23

Extra resources

Porges, S.W. (2011). *The polyvagal theory: Neurophysiological foundations of emotions, attachment, communication, and self-regulation (Norton series on interpersonal neurobiology)*. WW Norton & Company.

References for page 32	
* Ref no.	Where to find it in the reference text
1	p300, p310, p351,
6	p907
7	p814, p878
11	p9-11, p23, p25
16	p69
18	p240-257
21	p56, p114-8
34	p79-81, p124, p133
35	p118, p142, p231, p305
36	p321, p431, p434, Sec 3.10, Sec 7.13-7.14
41	p9, p28-29
48	p268-279
49	P23
50	p473-500
51	p38, p138
56	article
Extra resources	
'Can you think yourself into a different person?': Article by Dr Sarah McKay 'Neuroplasticity. Keep it fun, keep it simple': Slides by Dr Loretta Breuning	

* Ref no. See pages 47-49 for the list of references this number relates to. For example, Ref no. 1 is reference 1 on page 47 (*Amthor, F. (2016). Neuroscience For Dummies* (2nd ed.). *John Wiley and Sons, Inc.*).

References for page 33	
* Ref no.	Where to find it in the reference text
3	p289-303
1	p195
8	p153-179
9	article
10	throughout
24	p353-373
25	throughout
26	p6-41

References for page 35	
* Ref no.	Where to find it in the reference text
29	from 27:10mins
35	p143
58	throughout

References for page 34	
* Ref no.	Where to find it in the reference text
1	p299-300
2	p10-22
12	throughout
25	p34
30	throughout
33	p86, throughout
36	p415
41	chapter 8
55	podcast
Extra resources	
Brown, P.C., Roediger III, H.L. & McDaniel, M.A. (2014). *Make it stick: The science of successful learning*. Harvard University Press.	
Clear, J. (2023). *Atomic Habits By James Clear*. Dharman.	
Grant, A. (2023). *Hidden Potential*. Ebury Publishing	

References for pages 36-43
Lyall, D. (2021). *Enhancing the efficacy of coaching: defining and exploring reflexive hindering using an applied neuroscience approach and a developed infographic*. Doctoral thesis, University of Wales Trinity St David Research Repository. https://repository.uwtsd.ac.uk/id/eprint/2442
Specific references
Ekhtiari, H., Rezapour, T., Aupperle, R.L. & Paulus, M.P. (2017). Neuroscience-informed psychoeducation for addiction medicine: A neurocognitive perspective. *Progress in brain research, 235,* 239-264.
Miller, R. (2016). Neuroeducation: Integrating brain-based psychoeducation into clinical practice. *Journal of Mental Health Counseling,* 38(2), 103-115.
Shabi, A., & Whybrow, A. (2019). Ontological coaching. In S. Palmer & A. Whybrow (Eds.), *Handbook of coaching psychology: A guide for practitioners* (2nd ed., pp. 219-228). Routledge.

Ref no.	Reference List
1	Amthor, F. (2016). *Neuroscience For Dummies* (2nd ed.). John Wiley and Sons, Inc.
2	Bachkirova, T. (2009). Cognitive-developmental approach to coaching: an interview with Robert Kegan. *Coaching: An International Journal of Theory, Research and Practice,* 2(1), 10-22.
3	Barnard, L.K. & Curry, J.F. (2011). Self-compassion: Conceptualizations, correlates, and interventions. *Review of general psychology,* 15(4), 289-303.
4	Barrett, L.F. (2018). *How emotions are made: the secret life of the brain*. Pan Books.
5	Barrett, L.F. (2020). *Seven and a half lessons about the brain*. Houghton Mifflin Harcourt.

Ref no.	Reference List
6	Barto, A., Mirolli, M. & Baldassarre, G. (2013). Novelty or Surprise?. *Frontiers in psychology*, 4, 907. DOI: 10.3389/fpsyg.2013.00907
7	Bear, M.F., Connors, B.W. & Paradiso, M.A. (2016). *Neuroscience: exploring the brain* (4th ed.). Wolters Kluwer.
8	Boyatzis, R. (2013). Coaching With Compassion: Inspiring Health, Well-Being, and Development in Organizations. *Journal of Applied Behavioral Science*, 49(2), 153-179.
9	Boyatzis, R. (2015). Coaching With Compassion vs Coaching For Compliance. *Leaderonomics*. https://www.leaderonomics.com/articles/personal/coaching-with-compassion
10	Boyatzis, R., Smith, M. & Van Oosten, E. (2019). *Helping People Change: Coaching with Compassion for Lifelong Learning and Growth*. Harvard Business Press.
11	Brown, P., Kingsley, J. & Paterson, S. (2015). *Fear-free Organization*. Kogan Page.
12	Brown, P.C., Roediger, H.L. & McDaniel, M.A. (2014). *Make it stick*. Harvard University Press.
13	Buzsáki, G. (2004). Neuronal Oscillations in Cortical Networks. *Science*, 304(5679), 1926-1930.
14	Carlson, N.R. (2014). *Foundations of behavioral neuroscience* (9th ed., International ed.). Pearson.
15	Churchland, P.S. (2014). *Touching a nerve: our brains, our selves*. W.W. Norton & Company.
16	Cozolino, L.J. (2017). *The neuroscience of psychotherapy: healing the social brain* (3rd ed.). W.W. Norton & Company.
17	Curran, A.S. (2008). *The little book of big stuff about the brain: the true story of your amazing brain*. Crown House Publishing.
18	Dayan, P. (2012). Twenty-Five Lessons from Computational Neuromodulation. *Neuron*, 76(1), 240-257.
19	Dehaene, S. (2014). *Consciousness and the brain: Deciphering how the brain codes our thoughts.* Penguin.
20	Doidge, N.M. (2008). *The Brain That Changes Itself: stories of personal triumph from the frontiers of brain science* (2nd ed.). Scribe.
21	Eagleman, D. (2015). *The Brain*. Canongate Books.
22	Feinstein, J.S., Adolphs, R., Damasio, A. & Tranel, D. (2011). The Human Amygdala and the Induction and Experience of Fear. *Current biology*, 21(1), 34-38.
23	Fox, K. (2006). The smell report. *Social Issues Research Centre*, *334*, 385-400.
24	Gilbert, P. (1998). Evolutionary psychopathology: Why isn't the mind designed better than it is?. *British Journal of Medical Psychology*, 71(4), 353-373.
25	Gilbert, P. (2013). *The compassionate mind: a new approach to life's challenges*. Robinson.
26	Gilbert, P. (2014). The origins and nature of compassion focused therapy. *British Journal of Clinical Psychology*, 53(1), 6-41.
27	Fox News. (2015, October 27). Girl born without a brain is now 6 years old, family seeks support. *Fox News*. http://fxn.ws/1uaqO04
28	Glaser, J.E. (2016). *Conversational intelligence: How great leaders build trust and get extraordinary results*. Bibliomotion, Inc.
29	Goleman, D. (2013). Daniel Goleman on Focus: The Secret to High Performance and Fulfilment. *You Tube*. https://youtu.be/HTfYv3IEOqM?feature=shared
30	Hawkins, P. & Smith, N. (2018). Transformational Coaching. In Cox, E., Bachkirova, T. & Clutterbuck, D. (Eds) *The complete handbook of coaching* (3rd ed., pp. 231-246). Sage Publications Inc.
31	Holland, J.H. (2014). *Complexity: a very short introduction*. Oxford University Press.
32	Hwang, K., Hallquist, M.N. and Luna, B. (2013). The development of hub architecture in the human functional brain network. *Cerebral Cortex*, 23(10), 2380-2393.

Ref no.	Reference List
33	Kegan, R. & Lahey, L. (2002). *How the way we talk can change the way we work: seven languages for transformation*. John Wiley.
34	LeDoux, J. (2002). *Synaptic self: how our brains become who we are*. Viking Penguin.
35	LeDoux, J. (2016). *Anxious: Using the Brain to Understand and Treat Fear and Anxiety*. Penguin.
36	Luo, L. (2016). *Principles of neurobiology*. Garland Science.
37	Macknik, S.L., Martinez-Conde, S. & Blakeslee, S. (2012). *Sleights of mind: what the neuroscience of magic reveals about our brains*. Profile.
38	Merker, B. (2007). Consciousness without a cerebral cortex: A challenge for neuroscience and medicine. *The Behavioral and brain sciences*, 30(1), 63-81.
39	New, S.A. (2017). *How your brain works: inside the most complicated object in the universe*. John Murray.
40	O'Hare, J.K. et al. (2017). Striatal fast-spiking interneurons selectively modulate circuit output and are required for habitual behavior. *Elife*, 6.
41	O'Mara, S. M. (2018). *A brain for business - a brain for life: how insights from behavioural and brain science can change business and business practice for the better*. Palgrave Macmillan.
42	Pinker, S. (2015). *How the mind works*. Penguin.
43	Porges, S.W. (2004). Neuroception: A subconscious system for detecting threats and safety. *Zero to Three* (J), 24(5), 19-24.
44	Porges, S.W. (2007). The polyvagal perspective. *Biological psychology*, 74(2), 116-144.
45	Porges, S.W. (2017). *The pocket guide to the polyvagal theory: The transformative power of feeling safe*. WW Norton & Co.
46	Puder, D. (n.d.). Episode 023: Emotional Shutdown - Understanding Polyvagal Theory. *Psychiatry& Psychotherapy*. https://www.psychiatrypodcast.com/psychiatry-psychotherapy-podcast/polyvagal-theory-understanding-emotional-shutdown
47	Ramachandran, V.S. (2012). *The tell-tale brain: Unlocking the mystery of human nature*. Random House.
48	Schomaker, J. & Meeter, M. (2015). Short-and long-lasting consequences of novelty, deviance and surprise on brain and cognition. *Neuroscience & Biobehavioral Reviews*, 55 268-279.
49	Schultz, W. (2016a). Dopamine reward prediction error coding. *Dialogues in clinical neuroscience*, 18(1), 23.
50	Schultz, W. & Dickinson, A. (2000). Neuronal coding of prediction errors. *Annual review of neuroscience*, 23(1), 473-500.
51	Seth, A., Frith, C.D. & Bekinschtein, T. (2013). *30-second brain: the 50 most mind-blowing ideas in neuroscience, each explained in half a minute*. Icon.
52	Seung, S. (2013). *Connectome: how the brain's wiring makes us who we are*. Penguin.
53	Shabi, A. (2015). Ontological Coaching by Aboodi Shabi. *Crowe Associates Ltd*. http://www.crowe-associates.co.uk/wp-content/uploads/2013/10/Ontological-Coaching-article.pdf
54	Siegel, D.J. (2011). *Mindsight: The new science of personal transformation*. Oneworld Publishing.
55	Smith, N. & Hawkins, P. (2017). Transformational Coaching. *Renewal Associates*. https://www.renewalassociates.co.uk/resources/videos/
56	Storr, W. (2015). Can You Think Yourself Into A Different Person?. *Huffington Post*, 18(11),
57	Swaab, D.F. (2014). *We are our brains: from the womb to alzheimer's*. Allen Lane.
58	Tan, C. (2018). *Search inside yourself*. HarperCollins.
59	Shaw J (2020). Do False Memories Look Real? Evidence That People Struggle to Identify Rich False Memories of Committing Crime and Other Emotional Events. *Frontiers in psychology*, *11*, 510535.
60	Toates, F. (1996). The embodied self: A biological perspective. In Stevens, R. (ed.) *Understanding the self* (1st ed., pp. 35-88). Sage Publishing Inc.
61	Vinod, A. (2015, July 1). Why Do Dogs Have Such a Great Sense of Smell?. *Science ABC*. https://www.scienceabc.com/nature/animals/why-dogs-sense-of-smell-is-so-good.html

Printed in Great Britain
by Amazon